Steps to Loving You, Creating Positive Changes

Trish Scoular, RPC

Steps to Loving You, Creating Positive Changes Copyright © 2017 by Trish Scoular

All rights reserved. No part of this book may be used or reproduced in any manner whatsoever without written permission except in the case of brief quotations embodied in critical articles or reviews.

Disclaimer: Although the author and publisher of this book have made every effort to ensure that the information in this book was correct at press time, the author and publisher do not assume and hereby disclaim any liability to any party for any loss, damage, or disruption caused by errors or omissions, whether such errors or omissions result from negligence, accident, or any other cause.

Back Cover Photo Credit Regina Akhankina
www.couture.photography

Published by Prominence Publishing
www.prominencepublishing.com

ISBN: 978-1-988925-14-1

First Edition: December 2017

Dedication

This book is dedicated to all those who have taught me the importance of Loving Self!

We live in a world of people who are busy, often caring for others and not enough about themselves.

The purpose of this book is to help you understand and work through some of your own personal issues. Often the messages that keep us stuck are core and limiting beliefs.

Thank you to my Family and Friends who always encourage me to do better, that see the best in who I am and help me to succeed. Stepping outside my comfort zone has pushed me to try new things and the result has seen positive changes. The importance of Self Love is to always nurture ourselves by addressing those issues where we remain stuck, when we look closer at what they are, we begin to recognize patterns that can be changed.

Many thanks to my publisher Suzanne for all her support and guidance, plus the Oceanside Women's Business Network, the Greater Nanaimo Chamber of Commerce and the Ladysmith Waterfront Art Gallery, all of where I am a member.

TABLE OF CONTENTS

Dedication iii
Introduction 1
Slaying Dragons: Getting to the Root of Your Beliefs 10
Defining Who You Are 21
Draw the Line: Creating Boundaries that Work 27
Know Your Lingo: Communication Styles 31
Victorious Crusader: Positive Outcomes to Difficult Relationships 37
Spa For One: Loving Self/Care/Respect 41
Courageous Beauties: Finding Your Voice 48
Building Healthy Relationships 55
Overcoming Co-dependency 58
Sparkle Your Fashion: Defining What Makes YOU Unique 64
In Closing 73
About the Author, Trish Scoular 74

Introduction

Steps to Loving You is about a journey we are meant to take towards loving self. If we don't take that time to resolve our issues, we will remain stuck and repeat the same patterns while falling short of our dreams. Many women often find themselves not believing enough in who they are! They're either in a complacent relationship, single and want to have a man, stuck in a job where they are not happy, or other circumstances that have made them feel this way. They have been bullied, have no voice, show a lack of confidence, feel abandoned, homeless, frustrated, low self-esteem, angry and bitter. They desire to find tools they can use that will help them believe in themselves again; so they can move beyond their pain and feel fulfilled in all they do.

My journey has been one of similarity in which I can understand on many levels. It hasn't been easy these past 20 years, leaving me with the thought of giving up and not caring about myself or others. It wasn't until I decided to make different choices that I was finally able to make the change I desired. I was tired of feeling like I was going around in circles and getting nowhere, often banging my head against the wall or feeling frustrated because I wasn't being heard. It wasn't entirely about myself that I chose to finally stand up to a bully! It was because of many others who had also found themselves in a situation like mine and were mostly women.

I have finally healed seven years later, after nurturing my wounds and working on the inside. Asking why I hated myself, why these things always seem to happen to me, and why didn't people like me? It was a lonely time in my life, one that made me look at my friends, the people I was dating and why I kept repeating similar patterns while attracting all the wrong men. I went back to school and graduated with a Diploma in Applied Psychology and Counselling. Counselling was always an interest of mine and being a listener; I heard many of the same stories. I took steps to remove old habits, mixed messages that were on repeat, friends who kept me from growing and often feeling bad about myself. Going back to school helped me to work through my issues while discovering why certain things happened the way they did.

I discovered an art community where I share my passion for art while finding support and friendship there. It was in discovering myself that I learned to love myself more. Growing up I was often the fixer, the social worker, encourager, and listener. It was in my upbringing I was taught to believe that I was to love others as I love myself, but after some bad experiences, that perception was altered. I wasn't going to be a doormat and realized I needed to set boundaries, especially when NO was a word people didn't seem to understand. Most of my life I was afraid of hurting other's feelings until I realized that they weren't concerned about hurting mine, but instead of responding I reacted which didn't always bring about positive results. I also was taught to love my neighbor as myself, while quickly discovering that people didn't all love me the same way back. I always saw myself as a person who got along with others and was easy to deal with. It was the realization that not all people share the same goals, thinking, and values as we do. I also allowed myself to compromise in situations that made it much easier than to fight, creating an enabler in me and a co-dependent instead.

Learning to love myself was becoming something of the past and friends I had known soon drifted away. Years later I got in touch with an old friend who was still upset that I had chosen to adapt rather than stand and be strong like I was before I left Vancouver. I never realized that I was choosing to adapt because to me it seemed like the reasonable choice at the time. I was tired of feeling like I was not going to find love from a man so dated ones I knew would never last. Over time it left me feeling angry, bitter and in the end never wanting to date again.

While recreating my story has given me much more pleasure in life, I have also found a renewed joy in serving others in my business. Rather than feeling like I was constantly being taken advantage of which at one time I was, I have a much deeper connection to others through empathy, rely more on my intuition than second guessing myself like I had for years. I now have tools that helped me to discover and confirm my purpose, experiencing more joy and fulfillment in life. As a Counsellor, I can help you overcome depression, anxiety, limiting and core beliefs, plus co-dependency. By not adapting to what others want, you can choose to live your own life and feel happiness, which is important for us all.

The reason I wrote this book was to help women and girls resolve those deeper issues that were keeping them stuck. Its purpose is to give you the tools to help you take control of your life. I have provided questions that will guide you in that process and assist you in discovering positive results. This is a workbook so you can record your answers, and slowly begin to see patterns that were hidden.

Do you find yourself stuck and repeating the same patterns?

_____
_____
_____
_____
_____
_____
_____

What steps have you taken to make a change in your life?

_____
_____
_____
_____
_____
_____
_____

Steps to Loving You, Creating Positive Changes will teach you how to love others by loving yourself first. A journey that will sometimes bring you full circle to places you have been and moved away from. It helps you discover your gifts, talents, and desires, often giving validation where we needed it. It is a journey that guides you to fulfillment! I want to help you re-write your life story, that will have you no longer limiting yourself by what others think and your thoughts about who you are.

I have re-written my story which has left me stronger and with a strength that comes from within. A core belief of where I am now, rather than where I was. No longer limiting myself based on what others think of me. I have discovered that life with purpose is essential, whether that be as a Mother, or starting a movement that will change lives or finally starting your education no matter what age you are.

I have a deeper compassion than before having struggled with bankruptcy, welfare, bad relationships, infertility, chronic pain, depression, and bullying.

Understanding now that I have the tools to overcome my own issues when they arise while helping others. I remind my clients to honour their feelings and not push them aside like we often do. These cycles we experience can be broken, helping to discover a much happier person that is fulfilled and prosperous.

The goal is living a life, you have always dreamed of and are confident in. I encourage women and girls to look at themselves, rather than focus on other people. I suggest that they do something that brings them joy and to set aside 30 minutes 3x a week to begin. We look at empathy, communication styles, overcoming self-esteem/confidence issues, boundaries, loving your unique self with tools that can be applied every day.

My acronym is: LOVING SELF

Listening

Observing

Vulnerability

Inspiring

Nurturing

Genuine

Sensitive

Empathy

Loving

Friend

My mother tells me I was always the kind of kid who took others under my wing and had empathy. I would listen to my friends and my family while encouraging them. Like I mentioned I was a counselor, social worker, and fun loving girl to have around. It's no wonder I have chosen the path I've been on, going into acting and becoming a hairdresser/makeup artist too. I love to learn and being creative is important to me. These skills have allowed me to be the person I am today. Learning fulfills my mind, and the creative side an outlet.

It's not easy being empathic; sometimes you take on people's pain without understanding why or where it originates from. You may think this sounds crazy, but I remember sitting at work and having this revolving pain that circulated my abdomen, where my gall bladder was. I left work early and headed to the walk-in clinic. After an examination, my doctor said there was nothing wrong with me, so I went home. When I returned to work the next day explaining what had happened; a co-worker said she had that exact pain, was needing to have surgery, and waiting for a date. It is a gift giving you much more compassion and kindness for other people. It can be a burden too, taking on the weight of the world when you don't have too.

What gifts or talents do you possess that you aren't using to your fullest?

_____
_____
_____
_____
_____
_____
_____

In what areas could you use these gifts or talents?

_____
_____
_____
_____
_____
_____
_____

What do you want to accomplish in your life? How can you use these gifts/talents to succeed?

_____
_____
_____
_____
_____
_____
_____
_____

Each of us, I believe, have been given gifts we can use to help each other. We all have a story to tell, and a purpose for why we get up every day. Please write here what you feel those are:

_____
_____
_____
_____
_____
_____
_____

A purpose is something we all need, and when we lose that purpose, we find ourselves wanting to give up, experience depression and not feeling fulfilled in anything we do. My goal with this book is to help you understand and to work through some of your issues. I want to take you on a journey of hope, one that will leave you wanting more of what you need.

Chapter One

Slaying Dragons: Getting to the Root of Your Beliefs

Core beliefs are messages we were often told as children that become implanted into our nervous system. They could have been avoided had we known and let go of them earlier. It's when we become adults and feel stuck, that we find ourselves needing to re-visit them. What our life is now, may not resonate with what you believed about yourself then. Often they result in attachments that we have emotionally connected with other people, events, and circumstances. Beliefs that are assumptions we have about ourselves, others and how we expect things should be in our world. When that doesn't happen, we often become upset, angry and disappointed. Core beliefs involve theories, ideas, and explanations about how we think things are, and what we think they should look like. We use these beliefs as anchors to help us express our understanding of the world we live in.

They are what form the foundation and help us to feel that sense of certainty, giving us peace of mind that will often reduce stress, anxiety, and fear. Keep in mind that these are not facts but are usually interpreted as facts, because they have been deeply entrenched. When we look back at our childhood experiences rather than how our life is now, we base our conclusions on those experiences. Discovering what may have served us then, is no longer serving us now.

CLIENT STORY

"My biggest fear with going to counselling was the stigma. 'Why couldn't I figure out my problems?' Also with, what the Counsellor would think of me, I don't talk openly about my true feelings; so I was nervous, but Trish was friendly and open. She helped me to feel as though I was talking to a friend. I never felt any judgment from her; it was freeing. The biggest benefit I realized was that I was struggling with my issues of depression and anxiety, stemming from not being truthful. I was always worried about others' opinions about my life; I realized I just did what people wanted me to do against my own happiness. My favourite part was the incorporation of Reiki and energy healing; it brought forth so much trapped emotion. Also working with the worksheets, there was just so many realizations brought for a while working with cognitive therapy. I would recommend Trish and Love From the Inside to my friends, strangers, anyone who will listen and benefit from what she has to offer. Our sessions were life-changing for me, I still have my moments and will go back to Trish at any time."

About 95% of our beliefs influence the decisions we make and the actions we take. These are the foundations of our self-concept and determines how you view yourself, in relation to others around you. They are labels you create, limitations and expectations of yourself which they are built on. Self-esteem are your feelings about those things you know.

Is there a core belief that is keeping you stuck in a pattern that hinders where you are now? If so, please write them here:

_____
_____
_____
_____
_____
_____
_____

Can you remember the first time that message occurred? It's good to look at what happened, discovering if they are similar to what is currently happening now.

_____
_____
_____
_____
_____
_____
_____

Once we identify what that message was, we are able to change it. Please write what you think it was here:

_____
_____
_____
_____
_____
_____
_____

WHAT LIMITS YOU?

Limited beliefs are goals that align with your life's purpose; they include our six human needs, values, and self-concept. It's when they don't align with our beliefs that we begin to self-sabotage. This is why it's important to be clear on what you want and not compromise because you feel less than, desperate or lonely. Your goals, objectives, and outcomes are key to discovering what it is that is holding you back. It is these beliefs that have been set that are most likely attributing to your success as well.

I understand how limiting beliefs can happen. Often we know what we want, but don't feel we deserve what we want. When something good happens, we tell ourselves that recurring message of why it would not be good for me, why do they want me to change, why is he/she being so kind and wanting me to do better? I believe we feel comfortable with certain people and a lifestyle that we become afraid to change. Afraid of losing what we have, in a gain of something better. This is when we self-sabotage; by jumping into relationships, and jobs we often end up feeling like we settled, in place of the joy we could have.

Please answer the following questions:

A). *What do you want to achieve in the next three months?*

_____
_____
_____
_____
_____
_____
_____

B). *What goals would you like to achieve in the next 6 - 12 months?*

_____
_____
_____
_____
_____
_____
_____

C). *What do you feel is currently keeping you from achieving those goals?*

D). When are you the most authentic person? Do you find that you change to please others? Sometimes finding a mentor can help us achieve our dreams. Is there someone you can think of you respect, you could learn from?

E). What are the benefits of letting go?

F). What is it specifically you would like to change?

G). What specific beliefs are not working for you?

H). What beliefs are preventing you from achieving your desired outcome?

To make these changes, we need to invest in them, following through with the action we are committed to taking. A certain belief you may have might be useful in a particular situation, but not necessarily with the goal, you are currently trying to achieve. Which should raise a flag around what that belief is, that may still linger. If you find it isn't helping you and only hinders progress, it's time to look at what could most likely be a limiting belief.

Recently I attended a workshop on finding your soulmate. I was reminded of one belief that had shut me down and kept me from wanting to date anymore. After 30 years in the dating game, I had concluded that all men were players, non-committal, jerks, compartmentalizers, and users. These were based on my own experiences and now blocking progress from wanting to continue. It was apparent I was attracting all the wrong ones, was in the wrong circles and perhaps those core beliefs I had that I was not good enough, pretty enough or smart enough still resonated. It's how I was feeling then, feeling now and every guy I had dated seem to tell me the same thing since "I had low self-esteem!"

A) *What experiences have you had that limit you from moving forward in a specific area?*

_____
_____
_____
_____
_____
_____

B) Is there an emotion that is attached to your experiences (a trigger) that reminds you that life is how you see it now? Explain here.

C) Letting go of FEAR is like cleaning house. Even though it is hard to let go of stuff, it is necessary in order to move forward and make the changes we desire. What ideas or thoughts have become fear-based, leaving you stuck and afraid of moving on?

D) What are you afraid of most, that you must let go of? Why?

_____
_____
_____
_____
_____
_____
_____

Some ways people can limit their beliefs are by making excuses, complaining, having negative thoughts, bad habits, self-talk, jumping to conclusions, making assumptions, your fears or worries, procrastination, and perfectionism. The three things that will help you create a set of empowering beliefs in achieving your goals are responsibility, commitment and now. It's important you allow them to become new thoughts, which can absorb into your brain and make them effective.

Chapter 2

Defining Who You Are

We have all been given gifts and talents to help us fulfill a purpose in life. These often give you joy; they calm your moods, relax your mind and create happiness on many levels. These are attributes that we sometimes stuff because we don't want to recognize them and don't value that part of ourselves. This can happen because we have believed what others have said. Recognizing and embracing these qualities can help you succeed! It's important to define who we are! By loving self, we begin to feel more confident and start to dress in a style that makes you feel good about yourself, bringing a higher level of joyful satisfaction. Often we want to be like someone else, so we dress and talk like them, rather than being who we genuinely are. We compare, instead of accept self and others for who they are, so we put them down instead with the hope of making ourselves feel better. Do we feel better though?

1) What makes you unique?

_____

_____

_____

2) What qualities make you feel special?

A). What value do you place on each talent?

B). What gifts do you have that you aren't using to their fullest?

_____
_____
_____
_____
_____
_____
_____

C). What messages have they conveyed in your mind, heart and soul? Positive/Negative?

_____
_____
_____
_____
_____
_____
_____

D). Were you ever told they weren't important or insignificant?

_____
_____
_____
_____
_____

E).   Who defines you? Yourself or Other People?

F). What three qualities do you feel happiest about having?

1.
2.
3.

G).   On a scale of 1 to 10, how would you rate yourself?   1 (least) and 10 (most)

H). Where do you think these messages stem from? Were they core or limiting beliefs?

_____
_____
_____
_____
_____
_____
_____
_____

I). What do you feel sets you apart from others?

_____
_____
_____
_____
_____
_____
_____
_____

J). What qualities do you like about yourself?

_____
_____
_____
_____
_____

K). What qualities don't you like about yourself?

L). Are you a people pleaser?

Chapter 3

Draw the Line: Creating Boundaries that Work

Boundaries are limits we define that separate us from others; it also promotes integrity. They help to create space for each other and consist of five components that include the spiritual, emotional, physical, sexual and relational. They're also red flags that tell us to stay away, often not understanding until later, why! A reason we should stop and pay attention rather than proceed.

Emotional boundaries are sets of feelings and reactions that belong to us. We have histories, values, goals, concerns, ideas, and perceptions that are ours. Nobody responds, reacts or perceives as we do. I had a client that was asking how to set boundaries with a friend who constantly puts her down. I suggested that it is always best to approach that person and ask them why they constantly choose to do so. Let them know it hurts your feelings and is not acceptable. If it continues, it is your choice whether to keep them in your life or whether to let them go. Sometimes the person may not know what they are doing until you tell them it's not okay.

Spiritual boundaries are when someone constantly tries to change our ideas, about what we believe in and how we choose to worship.

Sexual boundaries happen when we allow things that make us feel uncomfortable or forced upon when you said NO.

Relational boundaries are what we set while interacting with others, letting them know what is appropriate and what is not. It brings order to our lives and sets the line on how others will treat you.

We have developed boundaries since infancy. If you are from a healthy family, you were most likely taught to be independent and separate from others. You only learn about them by the way you were treated as a child, sometimes taught to let others walk all over you. They are something that can leave you open and with difficulties as you age.

A). What do you consider to be healthy boundaries?

_____
_____
_____
_____
_____
_____
_____
_____

B). What do you consider to be unhealthy boundaries?

_____
_____
_____
_____
_____
_____
_____
_____

C). How do they protect us?

_____
_____
_____
_____
_____
_____
_____
_____

D). How do you set your boundaries?

_____
_____
_____
_____
_____
_____
_____
_____

E). Do you respect others' boundaries? If not, why?

Chapter 4

Know Your Lingo: Communication Styles

One thing my parents taught me was always to be careful what I said. You never know what another might be going through, and could be surprised later on that you were wrong. You may end up feeling bad about the comment you made that was derogatory and untrue. The other value was how to treat other people despite their appearance and whether I liked them or not. I was taught empathy always putting myself in someone else's shoes. It was because of those teachings that I was able to understand and engage on a deeper level while building relationships with others.

I always assumed that others were like me in my beliefs and the way I connected would be similar. I discovered that this wasn't always the case. People I met also grew up in dysfunctional families where there was disrespect, abuse, and alcoholism, not that mine was perfect because in my immediate family these things did not occur. There was alcohol when my family got together, but for the most part, they were happy, singing and playing their instruments well into the night, like a lot of families, I'm sure. I only saw my father drink one or two when we were with relatives, never drunk and rarely did they yell. I understood in my later twenties that my Uncle had abused my cousins, which was quite a shock when I learned the truth about what had happened. Now my cousin who also is a Counsellor helps people around the world through their sexual abuse.

Sometimes we find ourselves having to adapt to others to fit into an environment we may not be accustomed too. It's never a good thing to change who you are, just to fit in even though it might seem easier going with the flow, instead of fighting it. I was worried about ending up like a family member who suffered five nervous breakdowns and another experiencing one, and every time I felt I was in an emotional crisis and there were a few moments when I was concerned. However, I was able to process what happened, and realize that all I can do is get up and keep going. I remember my Aunt telling me to not end up like her, she drank and smoked too much. She always worried about having had adopted her two children than being able to give birth, and that she was a terrible mother and they deserved better. All messages that were wrong in our mind, but real in hers.

When you start to accommodate and adapt to please others, it can damage your emotional and mental health. This can happen in any new situation that could include moving to a new place, starting a new job, moving to a new housing development and trying to make new friends. Finding a tribe of people you mix well with helps in new situations allowing you to build trust, friendship and honesty are important. Joining a club that you might have similar interests with would help with creating the kinds of friends you want to get to know.

What steps can you take to help you make healthy choices and create boundaries that are effective in any new situation?

It's important to understand how to communicate effectively so you can establish boundaries, have a healthy dialogue with others and know what style will be most effective in getting what you want. The four communication styles are: passive, passive-aggressive, aggressive and assertive.

A). What is your communication style?

B). Do you feel you are achieving positive results with your style of communicating? Why or Why not?

C). Of the four types of communication styles, which one do you use often?

D). What is your definition of passive? Give an example:

E). What is your definition of passive-aggressive? Give an example:

F). What is your definition of aggressive? Give an example:

G). What is your definition of assertive? Give an example:

_____
_____
_____
_____
_____
_____
_____
_____

H). What do you feel is the best communication style to use that will give you amazing results? Why?

_____
_____
_____
_____
_____
_____
_____
_____

Chapter 5

Victorious Crusader: Positive Outcomes to Difficult Relationships

Have you ever found yourself in a situation, where you are dealing with a difficult person? I am sure you like me, are no different and have. They are everywhere!! Often leaving you feeling like you will never win and will always have to rise above to overcome the objections these types of people seem to project your way. It's so bad it affects your job and wanting to find a new one, always finding ways of avoiding them, even calling in sick. It doesn't matter how nice you are; they just continue to make you feel less than you are.

People think that bullying is overrated, but it's not. 65% of the population in Canada are bullied every day. They are continually singled out, picked on and excluded from participating in various groups. They might be shy, different from others or new to the area or workplace. In telling my own story of being bullied, others opened up to me about their experiences too. The impact it left on them and the feeling of continual victimization. In Canada, laws exist in every Province but three. WorkSafe BC continually works with advocacy groups, government officials and employers to come up with solutions that fix the ongoing problem. (Source: Worksafe BC and RCMP Stats)

There are protocols in schools that assist students with anonymous reporting, and support for those that wish to face the bully and talk openly about it. It seems to be most effective with victim and bully, where tools and support can be given to both. With the bully, it is a learned behaviour, something that was ingrained since childhood. According to the RCMP, 60% of boys who frequently bully in elementary schools have criminal records by age 24, with the likelihood of alcohol or drug use.

Three types of bullying exist: physical, verbal and social. With cyber bullying as the most popular form, by sending out mean or threatening emails and text messages. Other embarrassing moments can be unwanted photos posted online, tricking someone to post personal information and then sending it to others. This kind of behaviour stays with someone 24/7, impacting all areas of their life. For the victim, the effects are damaging! Putting people in a place of isolation, low self-esteem, fearful, depressed, anxious, aggressive behaviours, missing school or work and lower grades. Often and most definitely among youth, suicide becomes the only option.

If you are a victim here are some tools to use: always keep a journal, walk away from online conversations, talk to a trusted adult, report it to the local police, school and employer. Report unwanted text messages to your local phone company, and cyber bullying to your social media site, and block the person responsible. 85% of bullying happens in front of people. 60% of the time it is stopped because someone intervenes.

1). Have you ever felt like a victim of bullying?

_____
_____
_____
_____
_____
_____
_____

2). Have you dealt with the issue? Does it still affect your self-esteem?

_____
_____
_____
_____
_____
_____
_____

3). What measures have you taken to help you through it?

_____
_____

4). If not, how does it still impact your life?

Chapter 6

Spa For One: Loving Self/Care/Respect

For those of us that can't afford a weekly or monthly spa day, there are things you can do at home. Self-care, respect, and pampering are critical after breaking up with a partner, job loss, death and moving to a new town. When we don't love our self, we neglect that part of ourself that needs nurturing. To me, a spa day is having a massage, getting a facial, sitting in a mineral pool, having a pedicure and a manicure, getting a Thai foot massage and the list goes on in a smorgasbord of delicious spa treats you can partake in. This makes for an expensive day, so how can we allow the same pampering on a budget?

One thing I did, was I learned some alternative therapy methods like reiki. There are lots of classes around that you can get this kind of training from. I don't use it with everyone, but sometimes I find it helpful in opening up clients to more discussion and break down barriers where they are stuck. There is also healing touch that works with energy. If you know anything about quantum physics, then you will understand how it works. You work with the aura of a person, and in that aura, you will discover breaks. I was a skeptic too at first until I took a class and was scheduled to attend but had a massive migraine. Having no way to contact the instructor I just showed up and explained why I couldn't be there. She said, "here sit down and let me work on you!" In 20 minutes the pain was gone, and I spent a weekend getting certified in Level One.

Mindfulness is also an easy technique to learn, one that promotes compassion and kindness, while allowing your mind to unwind while praying for others and self. It's a good way to start your day! You can also listen to white noise which can be downloaded as an app, or diffuse essential oils in the air and topically to your body where you feel the pain. Massage helps with muscle spasms while allowing a person to relax. There are several inexpensive courses you can take, that can be applied to your family and yourself. You can pick up face masks at the drug store and some Epsom salts, nail polish and foot lotion to massage into your feet afterward. If you're in a relationship have your partner assist with that.

A). What does a spa day look like to you?

_____
_____
_____
_____
_____
_____

B). What techniques are helpful for you in promoting relaxation?

C). When your mind is racing, what helps you to unwind?

D). How often do you pamper yourself?

E). What do you feel promotes healthy living?

Creativity and Loving Self/Respect

It's important to do something that gives you pleasure that can become a distraction for you. It will help get your mind off what's occurring. Knitting, crocheting, quilting, gardening, and other positive pursuits will help you. Art classes are good and don't take talent to enjoy one; they are therapeutic allowing you to access that side of your brain that we sometimes neglect. It helps in many areas of a person's life. I have listed some other creative hobbies you can try.

What can you do that would be a distraction from the pain you are feeling now? Or an emotion you are wanting to avoid?

Drawing a mandala helps to see yourself as whole and harmonious. Carl Jung suggested that creating a mandala fulfills our desire to live out our full potential, complimenting all aspects of self. The mandala first originated from the motifs discovered in ancient rock carvings found in Africa, North America and Europe. They often have distinct patterns that are circular, spiral and other patterns the person drawing them has created. Carl Jung was the first to use them in modern psychology. The word "mandala" in Indian traditions means center and circumference. It represents the nature of the psyche, bringing you again to center over and over. For kids, it helps to establish an identity, as a sense of self, begins to exist. They are spontaneous while teaching how to live in the moment of time and space, leaving room for change and growth.

I taught this idea to a group of chronic pain sufferers I belonged too. We discovered that it was a distraction, and enjoyed that playful hour to focus on something else that brought pleasure to the eye and also to the mind. How is this done? You begin by drawing a circle! You can include spheres and other shapes within the circle. Then you adorn them with jewels, clay stones, paint, pencil, flowers, sand, leather, wood, and cloth if you desire.

Art therapy is another tool that can help you work through any issues you may find difficult trying to express, that will unblock what lies hidden.   It helps with stress release, trauma, and illness.

Respecting Self!

Old patterns tend to surface when we find ourselves stuck. This can be due to a blockage, a limiting belief, or a subconscious sabotage that we don't feel we are deserving. It can also be a core belief if it was a message from our childhood that we didn't allow to lift. Instead, it imprinted in our nervous system. It's important to look at why they keep occurring so you can start living in the present moment rather than in the past, as I have mentioned in a previous chapter.

Habits such as smoking and overeating can be stopped. It takes 28 days to change a habit they say, for some 21 days. That means replacing your trigger with healthy choices and drinking lots of water. Smoking is a conscious decision, and understanding your triggers as to why you smoke, will help immensely when it comes to quitting. Try and keep a journal for 30 days, each time you find yourself wanting to smoke or overeat write it down and include the situation that occurred at that time. It will discover patterns and is also helpful when seeking therapy. Journalling is a great tool in problem-solving. The who, what, why, when and where questions we can ask ourselves in any dilemma will help us in finding the solution you were looking for.

Chapter 7

Courageous Beauties: Finding Your Voice

I think one of my own biggest challenges was standing up to strong people, especially women. Ones who seem to walk all over you, without giving you the opportunity to speak. I was the opposite of that; I was too afraid of hurting others' feelings that I walked away and said nothing instead. That is the right thing to do, but it's also important to let people know when they have overstepped a boundary. You don't have to do it harshly, you just need to be clear.

Standing up for ourselves is so important, I can't say that enough. If we don't stand up, we will only feel like a doormat over time and beat ourselves up for not saying something then. This will also become a passive-aggressive behaviour over time if we find we take it and then blow. So it's best to learn how to stand up before you explode. Standing up for ourselves also promotes self-respect, care, and love. People respect those who have boundaries that allow changes to occur.

Has there been a time where you felt like a doormat? If so, when and why?

_____
_____
_____
_____
_____
_____
_____

Do you find it difficult to stand up to others? If so, how?

_____
_____
_____
_____
_____
_____
_____

Do you know that the kind of tone we use gets different results? I think you do because we all use different tones at some point to be heard. If we speak quietly, we won't be heard, and people will struggle trying to hear us by getting frustrated in having too. If we speak too loud, then we are obnoxious. Being boisterous has it's place but also knowing how to use the right tone can show much more impact when dealing with a sick person, a friend who is depressed and needs understanding, or your kids that aren't listening and you're tired of asking what it is you want them to do.

The softer tones are for situations where you need compassion, empathy, and kindness. Middle tones are used for business conversations showing your confidence in a business meeting, casual conversation, and in everyday situations. Being loud is good for needing to be heard, perhaps while acting on stage, yelling at someone, so they don't get hurt or hit by a driver. Often, we find ourselves using tones that are not always appropriate, such as yelling at your children; yes it is necessary at times, but what are the words we are using in that tone and can they be hurtful? Will the impact over time of yelling, create better self-esteem or confidence in that person as they age? When we are angry we yell and sometimes words come out that are hurtful, do we say we are sorry? We should so the wrongs can be made right. Can there be forgiveness, yes?

Why do you feel having good self-confidence is important in the workplace?

_____
_____
_____
_____
_____

On a scale of 1 to 10 where do you rate yourself with confidence?

Do you think you suffer from low self-esteem? If so, why?

How do you express yourself when angry? Does it help or hinder?

Are you afraid to speak up? If so, why?

What do you feel is blocking you from standing up to others?

Do you rate yourself as extroverted or introverted? Why? Why do you think knowing this is important?

How important is having good self-esteem?

What kinds of tone do you use, and when? What is the impact of using that particular tone? Please explain.

Chapter 8

Building Healthy Relationships

I have always had good relationships with most people, and finding some commonalities that have made us friends. I feel it is important to take that approach instead of allowing our bias or discrimination to take over, leaving what could make a good friend despite their race, religion or culture. Yes, we are all trying to share our beliefs, but respecting another can make a huge difference in how we relate to each person we meet. It's about opening yourself up to learn, to accept and to care.

What bias do you have that is keeping you from making friendships with people different from yourself? Do you feel it is a core belief that has been ingrained? Is it because of media?

_____
_____
_____
_____
_____
_____
_____

It is true that we tend to stick with those we know, yet when we reach beyond that circle, we begin to grow even more than we had. It allows us to learn something new such as a language, a taste of ethnic food and a craft that we've never seen before. Perhaps sharing a song and learning a new way to dance. There is so much to experience, that life is never dull. Friendship is so important, almost like family and in some cases they are.

What motivates you to make friends with certain people?

_____
_____
_____
_____
_____
_____
_____
_____

Do you change as a result of choosing certain friends? If so, how? What impact does it make?

_____
_____
_____
_____
_____
_____

Do you consider your friends to be healthy or unhealthy relationships? Why?

So how do you build healthy relationships?

Chapter 9

Overcoming Co-dependency

I had never heard the term co-dependency until I lived in a small isolated town north of Vancouver. I was becoming friends with a woman who had rescued a man from up the coast. It turned out he wasn't the man of her dreams, and so much the opposite of what she wanted. It may have been infatuation, but the man ended up having problems that sucked her energy and others he met. She realized in time that she was co-dependent, a term from Co-Dependents Anonymous a group that resulted from AA in the USA. Having an alcoholic husband this made sense in how and why she selected people similar to him. What defines someone who is co-dependent is based on many things.

There are often denial patterns where people deny or minimize their feelings just to make others happy, suffer low self-esteem by judging themselves by words and thoughts that they are not good enough. They seek out other people's approval of those thoughts, feelings, and behaviours. They are compliant compromising their values, integrity to avoid rejection and other people's anger. They are loyal even in harmful situations; they are afraid to express different feelings because their value is greater on others' opinions. They accept sex as a substitute for love. There are control patterns, where they believe people aren't capable of taking care of themselves, so they constantly try to fix them instead. They freely offer advice and guidance without being asked, they lavish gifts and favours on those they care about. They have to be needed to have a relationship with others.

If you find yourself in this situation, you are not alone. Many people who have grown up in some dysfunctional family will experience co-dependency to some degree. Until we come to turns with this we will never change, our relationships will never be healthy, and there will be resentment and bitterness. This will always exist from constantly feeling disappointed. Until we realize the role we are playing our situation will never improve. I thought my mission in life was to rescue everyone, fix their needs when they were sharing problems and feeling hopeless, often time to have them feeling resentment instead. It wasn't until I chose to work on loving self, that my world began to change and in positive ways. I gave up that desire of wanting to fix, allowing my friends and family the choices they needed to make for their own life. Even though I knew they could do better, it was a journey they were on and none of my business to interfere, unless of course, they were harming self or others. That was a hard life lesson, but realizing that they knew best, it was easier to let go and accept that they may never change. Life came full circle allowing me to make those choices that were necessary to bring me to where I am now.

Where do we start?

We start by fixing self. It wasn't until I became a Counsellor that I realized why things were happening the way they had. I constantly asked myself: *What's wrong with me? If he/she changed everything would be all right... I keep getting into the same bad relationships...* These are constant questions that run through people's minds who suffer from co-dependency mild to extreme. I am happy I fell into the mild group and grateful for the light that came to mind.

I tried to justify that it was my religious upbringing that helped me be this way, trying to find something to blame rather than realizing I can't fix other people and I needed to take responsibility. I need to accept where they are and move on from them or encourage them when they are feeling low. Not taking on the weight of the world will bring my life fulfillment, joy, happiness, and self-confidence. No longer will people see me as having low self-esteem.

Managing Finances

Something that comes up continually with my clients is money. It seems that what we want from life is not always free and we have to pay for it. Expenses are getting higher, and our wages remain the same. Their partners don't want to help, and so women struggle to pay the bills, take care of the kids, go to school, buy a house and travel. What I suggest is a budget, and looking at how much they make, where their expenditures are and do they have enough to save.

There are many tools and apps out there that make budgeting easy; the problem is in the disciplinary of it that will make the change. Staying committed to what your budget is, to avoid the pitfalls. None of us are exempt it seems these days, as we are trying to live above our means as opposed to living within them.

Some of the things I have learned is volunteering at the theatre, a sports game or any other club you like to involve yourself in. You are not only helping the organization by being there, but you also get to enjoy what you love to attend but not necessarily what you can always afford. It gives a certain sense of satisfaction giving back while saving money.

I believe the relationship we have with money is based on how we feel about money. To some it is energy flowing through your hands, I like knowing that it sticks there while obtaining growth. For me, energy is working at not only helping yourself but helping others too, so the flow is always going and we are sharing our resources. The relationship we have with money determines our outcome in life. However sometimes we find ourselves in difficult situations, and that can be due to cutbacks at your place of employment, job loss of a spouse and illness too.

So how does a person plan for these kinds of circumstances when they haven't had enough to save even? Meeting with a financial planner is a good first step, so you can foresee what kind of money is good to put away for personal emergencies. Talking to your creditors can help as well, and most times are understanding which means they will be happy to work with. Here are some questions you can ask yourself.

A). What is your relationship with money?

_____
_____
_____
_____
_____
_____
_____
_____

B). Do you think there could be a limiting belief you might have around money?

_____
_____
_____
_____
_____
_____
_____
_____

C). What were you taught growing up about money? Did you understand what a budget was?

_____
_____
_____
_____
_____
_____
_____
_____

D) Do you have a budget? How is that working for you? Do you manage to save?

E). What are your beliefs about money?

Chapter 11

Sparkle Your Fashion: Defining What Makes YOU Unique

Beauty comes from within; what we add to that only highlights our feature qualities. The women in my family believe, "that a beautiful woman is a happy woman!" She is one that radiates through her smile and the sparkle in her eyes. She is a woman that is confident and secure in who she is, which comes from the reassurance of knowing that she is okay. When we talk about beauty, it reflects in her mind, her heart and her love of life, family, and friends. She speaks her truth and stands grounded never faltering the path that she has chosen.

When we talk about beauty, we recognize that all women love to dress up, and we sometimes will use make-up to accentuate certain parts of the face. We will apply perfume that entices and leave a scent that will linger in the minds of those around us. This would include hairstyles that suit our facial shape, makeup that brightens our eyes, lips, and cheeks. Fashion that shows that wild, fun side when we play or that more serious business attire we might rely on to get a job. These styles range from vintage, modern, chic, bohemian, classic and second hand. Then we accessorize with jewelry that adorn our outfits.

Beauty starts from within and includes our thoughts, feelings and the internal messages we believe while projecting out to the world. How we limit ourselves stops us from growing and being our authentic natural selves. You may have been told you weren't pretty, overweight and not smart enough to get a boyfriend or a husband. You may have been sexually abused, which has left you vulnerable with men and open to making choices that make you feel ashamed. You may suffer from depression, anxiety or a mental illness even, making you feel afraid.

This book I hope will help you to start a journey that will guide you to the woman you are, beautiful, loving, kind, caring, compassionate and a woman that is confident with positive self-esteem.

What makes you unique is the style you feel most confident in, and when you look in the mirror, you feel proud. You smile because you feel happy and fulfilled. It is each piece you have chosen that somehow resonates with how you feel about yourself. I am a mix of modern and vintage; I love the combination of both. In a radio interview, I was called a modern renaissance woman, one that has a diversity of skills that I can offer my clients. With my love of beauty, I also cherish my desire to learn. At a young age, my mother liked to encourage me in my pursuit of hairdressing. I would often sit on my father's lap at night and massage his head; I would practice up-dos and new hairstyles on my Barbie doll head I got for Christmas. My mother had me in ringlets and pretty dresses that my Grandmother made. We dressed nicely because we attended church, and other events because of my Father's involvement in clubs, hockey, and work. I was never much of a tomboy but a girl that loved to play dress up instead.

Yes, we cross-country skied and hiked, but I was always one of the slower one's that took my time and wasn't very athletic I have to say. I took hairdressing in school instead, often changing my hairstyle and the colour every other week. It is proven that having our hair done makes us feel so much better, I work in health care and notice an improvement in how one feels once that is done. The massage on the head as the shampoo and conditioner get rubbed in, stimulating those nerve endings, awakening the body and the mind. It also seems to affect our emotional and mental health. You have to remember also, that what catches your eye might not catch mine. What we think we like may not look good on us at all. That's the fun of trying on different styles of dress and having someone fit you properly for your body type, so you are not giving off messages, that may bring us negative attention.

There are different body types, apple, pear, banana, and hourglass. Height also plays a factor, going from petite to plus sizes. Our facial shapes are square, round, oval, oblong, pear, triangular and diamond. Shoes are based on comfort and size. Makeup is anywhere from natural to dramatic and stage. Oval is the best shape most people strive to create. But what makes us unique is our bone structure, ethnicity, facial shape, chin, forehead all of which should be vertically balanced. With a straight on view, we start at the hairline following to the inner brow, to the base of the nose and down to the chin all in proportion. Contour products like a liquid deeper shade of foundation, translucent powder and cream are used to refer areas of the face, and should always be a shade deeper from soft to medium.

Steps to Makeup Application:

1. Cleanse the face in an upward motion, repeating until all residue is gone. Include the neck and the ears, lips inward to the center. When cleansing eyes, sweep down over the lashes, then inward to the inner corner of the eyes. Never pull or stretch the delicate skin around your eyes.
2. Rinse your face at room temperature with water.
3. Protect with a moisturizer that creates a barrier.
4. Now that the face has been properly cleansed, we take a concealer, and lightly apply it to blemishes, under eye circles and other areas you want to diminish. You can also use a green concealer for dark circles and red patches which minimizes them more. Don't use thick amounts of concealer as it can accentuate your pores and other areas you don't like.
5. Then you apply the foundation, a shade that matches your skin tone. Using a wedged sponge will make it easier and will stop any contamination in the bottle that could occur, which is why I use a pump bottle. You dab the foundation around the face as you blend it in. Always use an upward motion when applying anything.

6. After that is done, you can begin to work on your eyes. The eyes are the windows of the soul and accentuating them will bring different results. There are many types of eye shadows you can purchase, and most come with the correct instructions on what colour to use first. You want to apply the darker one to the crease of the eye and a lighter one above under the brow, while applying the medium shade from eyelashes to the crease.
7. You can then apply an eyeliner. For the daytime choose one that will brighten but not be too dramatic. I use a blue one and only apply it under the eye where the lashes are from the outer eye coming in about half way. For night time you can apply it directly across the eye on the bottom and upper eye lashes.
8. Then use an eyelash curler to lengthen your eyelashes and make it easier to apply the mascara; use in upward motion from eyelid to tip of eyelash.
9. For the cheeks you want a darker contour colour that will give the illusion of some depth, usually it's below the cheekbone. Using a thicker brush you apply a small amount going up towards your hairline. You want it nice and natural. Buying a lighted mirror can help as it will give you the proper lighting you need for the type of day you are wanting.
10. Then take the blush color and apply it the same way except it is placed on your cheekbone instead.
11. Then you apply the lip liner and blend it in with your choice of lipstick.

12. You can use a loose powder or compact to lightly spread over your face. It works best in winter while the summer months can make it appear caked due to sweating. Always ask the cosmetics technician on the right one to buy so you aren't wasting your money. They are an excellent resource and often will give you a demonstration as well.

Make sure you drink eight glasses of water a day, avoid soaps and complete a deep cleanse at least 1x month. Have a professional facial if you can afford it, or try a homemade one at home.

Items for your makeup bag: velour powder puff, sponge, wedges and a natural sea sponge.

When we think about dress, what image are you trying to portray?

Do you know your body type and what flatters it?

Do you find the way you dress, flatter your body type? What kind of message does it give?

Do you dress for your age? If so, why? If not, why?

What value do you place on fashion and style?

Do you think it should affect your ability to get the job of your dreams? Why or why not?

_____
_____
_____
_____

In Closing

My hope is that if you purchased this book or received it as a gift, you will consider each chapter as a tool to begin your journey towards healing. It is meant to help you improve your relationship with yourself and can guarantee an improvement with those around you. It can sometimes be a painful journey, but knowing that we all can overcome any challenge, makes it worthwhile if you are willing to commit to 6 weeks when you begin.

I believe that we have the answers locked within, which is why I can assist you through those issues or beliefs that have kept you stuck. We will look at any core or limiting belief you may have from your childhood that could be affecting your adulthood

Book Your FREE Strategy Call

www.lovefromtheinside.com
250-900-7707

---

today. Book your 30-minute consultation today, so we can come up with a plan that will help address the issues you want to work on.

About the Author

Trish Scoular

Love From The Inside is about teaching people to love themselves first because we truly can't love another without doing the work. This is often a difficult thing to do for some people, especially if they have been given distorted messages that have stemmed from childhood, pre-teen years and even adulthood. These are messages that were damaging to our self-esteem from people we trusted and who were at times our peers, our parents and others in authority. Loving ourselves truly as we are is the first step towards finding happiness and discovering our true potential and deeper meaning in our relationships.

I am a Registered Professional Counsellor, and I work with children of aging parents, women, men, boys and girls. My clients have primarily come from a background of depression, difficult relationships, bullied, low self-esteem and confidence, anxiety and co-dependency with some budgeting issues too. I believe in person-centered theories because I think people have the answers to life's problems when they look within. Although it may not be a pleasant journey, the positive impact of doing so will bring much more awareness, positivity, happiness, and joy.

At my core is a heart that believes in helping others succeed. It is through my own experiences and education that I understand the cycles that occur, and we can sometimes find ourselves stuck in. I offer solutions that will help create awareness and look at what is at the core, or any limiting beliefs you may have about yourself. I come from a heart-centered place that provides compassion and empathy.

www.ingramcontent.com/pod-product-compliance
Lightning Source LLC
LaVergne TN
LVHW051155080426
835508LV00021B/2646